My First Pocket Guide

Montana

By Carole Marsh

Correlates with Montana's SSS Standards for Social Studies

The Montana Experience

The GALLOPADE GANG

Carole Marsh
Bob Longmeyer
Chad Beard
Cecil Anderson
Steven Saint-Laurent
Jill Sanders
Kathy Zimmer
Terry Briggs
Pat Newman
Billie Walburn
Jackie Clayton
Pam Dufresne
Cranston Davenport
Lisa Stanley
Antoinette Miller
Victoria DeJoy
Al Fortunatti
Shery Kearney

Published by GALLOPADE INTERNATIONAL

www.themontanaexperience.com
800-536-2GET • www.gallopade.com

Gallopade is proud to be a member of these educational organizations and associations:

NSSEA

ASCD

SHOPA MEMBER™
School, Home, & Office Products Association

Other Montana Experience Products

- The Montana Experience!
- The BIG Montana Reproducible Activity Book
- The Montana Coloring Book
- My First Book About Montana!
- Montana "Jography": A Fun Run Through Our State
- Montana Jeopardy!: Answers and Questions About Our State
- The Montana Experience! Sticker Pack
- The Montana Experience! Poster/Map
- Discover Montana CD-ROM
- Montana "Geo" Bingo Game
- Montana "Histo" Bingo Game

A Word From the Author... (okay, a few words)...

Hi!

Here's your own handy pocket guide about the great state of Montana! It really will fit in a pocket–I tested it. And it really will be useful when you want to know a fact you forgot, to bone up for a test, or when your teacher says, "I wonder . . ." and you have the answer–instantly! Wow, I'm impressed!

Get smart, have fun!

Carole Marsh

Montana Basics
Montana Geography
Montana History
Montana People
Montana Places
Montana Nature
Montana Miscellany

Montana Basics explores your state's symbols and their special meanings!

Montana Geography digs up the what's where in your state!

Montana History is like traveling through time to some of your state's great moments!

Montana People introduces you to famous personalities and your next-door neighbors!

Montana Places shows you where you might enjoy your next family vacation!

Montana Nature - no preservatives here, just what Mother Nature gave to Montana!

All the real fun stuff that we just HAD to save for its own section!

Who Named You?

Montana's official state name is...

State Name

Montana

Word Definition

OFFICIAL: appointed, authorized, or approved by a government or organization

Statehood: November 8, 1889

Montana was the 41st state to join the Union.

What's In A Name?

Montana got its name from the Latin word *montaanus* which means mountainous.

WHO Are You Calling Names?

State Nicknames

Montana is not the only name by which the state is recognized. Like many other states, Montana has some nicknames, official or unofficial!

Treasure State

Big Sky Country

Last Best Place

Land of Shining Mountains

Bonanza State

The rich mineral resources in western Montana earned it the nickname the "Treasure State."

State Capital: Helena

Helena began as a gold-mining camp called Last Chance Gulch in 1864. By the 1880s Helena was said to be the richest town in America, home to 50 millionaires. Now smaller and less assuming, Helena's main street is still called "Last Chance Gulch."

Helena's capitol building is built of sandstone and granite mined in Montana. A bronze statue on top of the copper dome represents Liberty.

Word Definition

CAPITAL: a town or city that is the official seat of government
CAPITOL: the building in which the government officials meet

State Government

Who's in Charge Here?

Montana's GOVERNMENT has three branches:

- **EXECUTIVE**: A governor, lieutenant governor, secretary of state, attorney general, superintendent of public instruction, state auditor, public service commissioners
- **LEGISLATIVE**: Two Houses: The Senate (50 members) House of Representatives (100 members)
- **JUDICIAL**: Supreme Court (a chief justice and six associate justices)

The number of legislators is determined by population, which is counted in the census every ten years; the numbers above are certain to change as Montana grows and prospers!

State Flag

Montana's current state flag was adopted in 1905. It features a version of the state seal on a field of blue, with the word *Montana* in gold across the top.

State Seal

The state seal of Montana features a sun rising over mountains, forests and the Great Falls of the Missouri River. The pick, shovel, and plow represent mining and farming. A ribbon at the bottom contains the state motto.

State Seal & Motto

Word Definition

MOTTO: a sentence, phrase, or word expressing the spirit or purpose of an organization or group

State Motto

Montana's state motto is... Oro y Plat

The motto is Spanish for "Gold an Silver," most likely on account of t gold and silver mined in Montan

Birds of a Feather

Western Meadowlark

This yellow, black, and white songbird has a "V" on its yellow breast.

The western meadowlark is very similar to the eastern meadowlark. However, the western meadowlark's song is louder and more flutelike.

Ponderosa Pine

The ponderosa pine is also called the western yellow pine. It has long needles in clusters of three. It usually grows between 80 to 200 feet (24 to 61 meters) tall.

State Flower

Bitterroot

A lovelier flower on earth was never sown.
—William Wordsworth

The bitterroot is most common in western Montana. It was discovered by Meriwether Lewis of the Lewis and Clark expedition. It was treasured by the American Indians, who ate its roots.

RIDDLE:
If the state flower got mixed up with the state bird, what would you have?

ANSWER: A bitter meadowlark who likes to eat roots—it could happen!

State Animal

Grizzly Bear

Because of their large size, grizzlies do not usually climb trees. However, they are very skilled in moving about mountains or thick forests.

The grizzly bear has a length of 8 feet (2.4 meters) on average and usually weighs around 800 pounds (363 kilograms). The color of the grizzly varies from reddish-brown to gray and even black. Grizzlies are massive in size, with broad, block-like heads and muscular bodies.

DUCK-BILLED DINOSAUR

Maiasaura peeblesorum

This duck-billed dinosaur is called *Maiasaura,* meaning "Good Mother Lizard." Several skeletons of adult *Maiasaura* have been found near nests containing eggs and young. *Maiasaura* ate plants and probably chewed its food, which most reptiles do not do.

State Song

Montana

In 1935, the state legislature adopted *Montana* as the official state song. Below are a few lines from the song.

Montana, Montana,
Glory of the West
Of all the states from coast to coast
You're easily the best.
Montana, Montana,
Where skies are always blue
M-0-N-T-A-N-A
Montana, I love you . . .

Blackdog

Blackdog soil is Montana's unofficial state soil. It provides some of the best farmland in the state. Wheat, barley, and alfalfa grow well in blackdog soil.

Yogo Sapphire

These blue gemstones have been highly prized since 800 BC. The Yogo Gulch Mine in Montana operated for 39 years, beginning in 1896. Yogo's sapphires are unique among the world's sapphires because of their uniform "corn-flower blue" color and their clarity.

Montana Agate

Agates are made of quartz crystals too small to be seen with the naked eye. Montana agates are most abundant along the Yellowstone River.

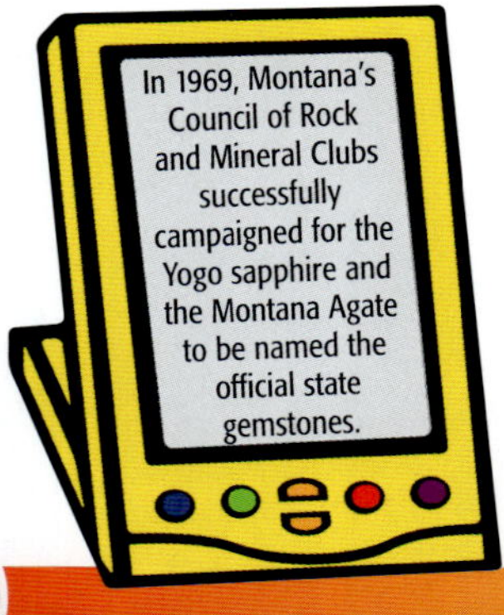

Bluebunch Wheatgrass

Bluebunch wheatgrass is found throughout the western U.S. and ranges from green to blue in color. It can grow to be 4 feet (1.2 meters) tall.

Blackspotted Cutthroat Trout

At the urging of two fly fishermen, Montana chose a state fish in February of 1977—the blackspotted cutthroat trout. Since it was on the threatened species list, many people felt that this attention could help the fish.

The State of Montana

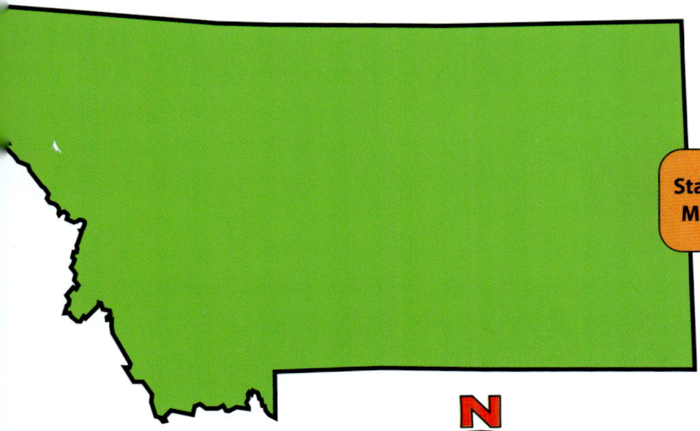

Montana is almost rectangular in shape. The Rocky Mountains in the western part of the state create a jagged boundary line.

State Location

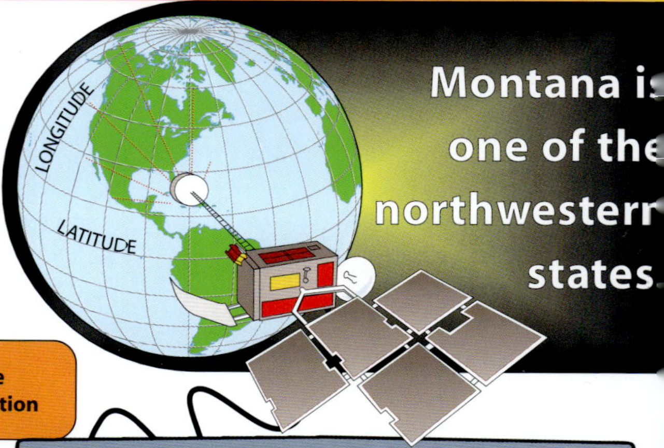

State Location

Word Definition

LATITUDE: Imaginary lines which run horizontally east and west around the globe
LONGITUDE: Imaginary lines which run vertically north and south around the globe

On The Border!

These border Montana:

States: Wyoming, Idaho, North Dakota, South Dakota

Country: Canada

I'll Take the Low Road...

Montana stretches 321 miles (517 kilometers) from north to south—or south to north. Either way, it's a long drive!

Total Area: Approximately 147,046 square miles (380,847 square kilometers)
Land Area: Approximately 145,556 square miles (376, 961 square kilometers)

Montana is 559 miles (900 kilometers) from east to west—or west to east. Either way, it's *still* a long drive!

You Take the High Road!

Highest & Lowest Points

Highest Point
Granite Peak—12, 799 feet (3,901 meters)

Granite Peak is named for the massive granite formations in the region. At this high elevation, snowstorms can occur any month of the year!

Lowest Point
Lincoln County along the Kootenai River—1,820 feet (555 meters)

I'm County-ing on You!

Montana is divided into 56 counties.

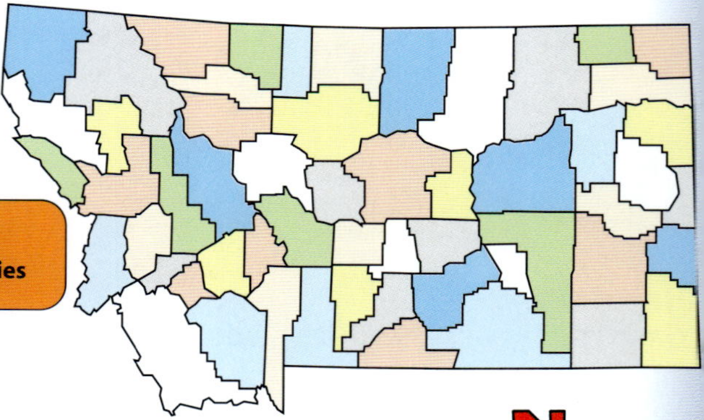

Word Definition

COUNTY:
an administrative subdivision of a state or territory

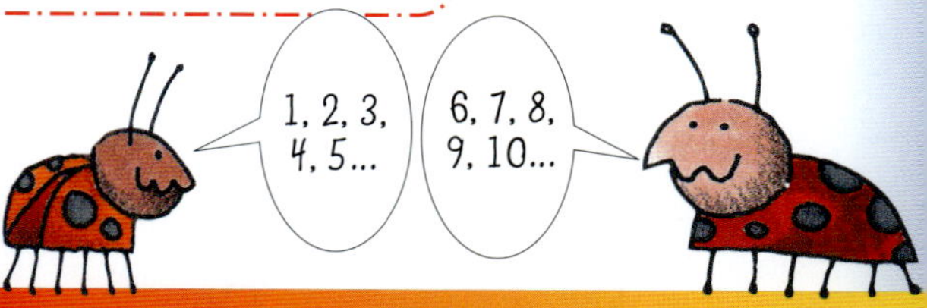

Natural Resources

It's All Natural!

Forests make up about 22,512,000 acres (9,110,606 hectares) in Montana.

Word Definition

NATURAL RESOURCES: things that exist in or are formed by nature

Minerals and rocks:

Coal
Copper
Silver
Gold
Lead
Zinc
Limestone
Gemstones

Montana is a major producer of Christmas trees, harvested both in the wild and on tree farms.

Weather, Or Not?!

Montana's temperatures average 8°F (13°C) in the winter and 87°F (31°C) in the summer.

Highest temperature: 117°F (47°C), Glendive, July 20, 1893, and again at Medicine Lake, July 5, 1937

°F=Degrees Fahrenheit °C=Degrees Celsius

Lowest temperature: -70°F (-57°C), Rogers Pass, January 20, 1954

Because of the diversity of Montana's geography, its climates are also diverse. The Continental Divide protects the western region from severe Canadian winds.

BACK ON TOP

Montana's topography includes the Great Plains and the Rocky Mountain region.

GREAT PLAINS: rolling plains once covered with tall, waving grasses; now carpeted with sagebrush and shortgrass; heavy farming and ranching land

ROCKY MOUNTAINS: Continental Divide separates these mountains from the Great Plains

Topography

Word Definition

TOPOGRAPHY: the detailed mapping of the features of a small area or district

Along the middle Missouri River and in the southeastern section of the U.S., badlands were cut by water and wind. Badlands include deep trenches and colorful rock formations.

King of the Hill

There are more than 50 Rocky Mountain ranges in Montana. Below are a few.

Bitterroot

Gallatin

Bridger

Flathead

Mission

Ruby

Lewis

Down The River

Here are some of Montana's major rivers:

- Missouri
- Yellowstone
- Bighorn
- Powder
- Tongue
- Shield
- Clark Fork
- Gallatin
- Jefferson
- Madison

Gone Fishin'

Major Lakes

- Flathead Lake
- Fort Peck Lake
- Bighorn Lake
- Canyon Ferry Lake
- Hungry Horse Reservoir
- Tiber Reservoir

Flathead Lake is Montana's largest lake, and the largest natural freshwater lake in the continental states west of the Mississippi.

Word Definition

RESERVOIR: a body of water stored for public use

ARE YOU A CITY MOUSE... OR A COUNTRY MOUSE?

Have you heard of these wonderful Montana town, city, or crossroad names? Perhaps you can start your own list!

MAJOR CITIES:

- Billings
- Bozeman
- Helena
- Great Falls
- Butte-Silver Bow
- Missoula

UNIQUE NAMES:

- Antelope
- Avon
- Big Arm
- Black Eagle
- Buffalo
- Circle
- Deer Lodge
- Hungry Horse
- Otter
- Pony

Transportation

Major Interstate Highways

I-94, I-90, I-15

Railroads

Montana contains 3,293 miles (5,300 kilometers) of railroad track.

Major Airports

Montana has principal airports in Billings and Great Falls. None of the state's 216 airports are considered busy by national standards.

Timeline

AD 1743	François and Louis Joseph de la Vérendrye explore the northern Great Plains
1803	Eastern Montana, as part of the Louisiana Purchase, becomes U.S. Territory
1805–06	Lewis and Clark travel through Montana on their expedition through the Northwest
1807	Manuel Lisa builds first fur-trading post; John Colter crosses the area of present-day Yellowstone National Park
1857	Gold is discovered at Gold Creek
1872	Congress establishes Yellowstone National Park, the country's first national park
1876	Sioux and Cheyenne Indians defeat George Custer in the Battle of Little Bighorn
1889	Montana becomes the 41st state
1894	Voters select Helena as the capital
1910	Congress establishes Glacier National Park
1916	Montana representative Jeannette Rankin becomes the first woman elected to the U.S. Congress
1924	Montana institutes a mining-license tax
1972	Montana voters approve a new state constitution
1985	Montana's Science and Technology Alliance is formed to find new ways to use the state's raw materials
1989	Montana celebrates its centennial
1996	Accused Unabomber terrorist Ted Kaczynski is seized in Montana
	On to the 21st Century!

Here come the humans!

Thousands of years ago, ancient peoples inhabited Montana. They may have originally come across a frozen bridge of land between Asia and Alaska. If so, they slowly traveled east until some settled in what would one day become the state of Montana.

The earliest people known to have lived in Montana were the Folsom people. They lived around 10,000 years ago and used a sling called an *atlatl* to hurl stone-pointed darts and spears at prehistoric bison.

Native Americans Once Ruled!

After the huge game animals began to disappear, the Yuman peoples began to settle in the far-western mountains of Montana. They left behind mysterious pictographs, or picture writings. After the Yumas came the Late Hunters. These people hunted deer, elk, and bison. Bison were very important in this culture. They were used for meat, clothing, shelter, and tools.

Land Ho!

Many early explorations of the American West were a result of the quest for a Northwest Passage—a water route through North America to the Pacific Ocean. Although it is not known for sure, most people believe that two brothers, François and Louis Joseph de La Vérendrye, were the first white men on Montana soil. They too were in search of a Northwest Passage.

Many traders and trappers later ventured into Montana, but it was another 60 years before an expedition was launched. President Thomas Jefferson appointed Meriwether Lewis and William Clark to lead an expedition that would travel all the way to the Pacific Ocean. One of their guides was a Shoshone Indian woman named Sacagawea, or "Bird Woman."

Home, Sweet Home

First came the fur traders, then the miners for the Montana Gold Rush. The growing number of people in the state required an organized government. Congress created the Montana Territory on May 26, 1864. A territorial legislature was created and a capital was named—Virginia City.

As settlers began to flood into Montana, they began claiming lands that had previously been hunted and lived on by American Indians. Several conflicts between settlers and Indians began to occur. U.S. Army troops were sent to Montana to protect the settlers and fight off the Indians.

FUR

The fur trade was important in early Montana. French fur trappers and traders often traded goods with the Indians and in return, they received beaver pelts and other furs. The furs were shipped to Europe to be made into clothing. Soon, fur trading companies built trading posts in Montana.

GOLD

When gold was found in California in 1848, people began searching for it in other territories. Around 1860, a few miners found small amounts of gold in Montana. Two years later, another gold strike occurred. The news spread and soon, hundreds of miners moved to places like Grasshopper Creek, Virginia City, Butte, and Last Chance Gulch (Helena).

Holy Man? Holy Cow!

According to legend, Father Pierre-Jean De Smet was asked by the Crow Indians to prove that he was a holy man. To do this, he was ordered to walk up to a bison (buffalo) in the wild. Calmly, Father De Smet walked up to the huge animal, patted its head, then returned unharmed to the Crow Indians!

Freedom! Freedom!

While Montana was being explored and harvested for furs by the French, settlers in the East were growing upset with their mother country, England. They felt that England ignored their ideas and concerns and taxed them too heavily. In 1775, the colonies went to war with England. This war was called the American Revolution, or the Revolutionary War. On July 4, 1776, the Declaration of Independence was signed, cutting ties with England. In 1783, the war ended and the colonies became the United States of America.

Slaves and Slavery

Early in eastern U.S. history, Africans were brought to work on plantations. Thousands of slaves were made to work on these large farms, growing and harvesting crops. Over time, some states abolished slavery, while others (the southern states) became more dependent on slavery. The fighting between the abolitionists and the slaveowners continued to mount. At this time, Montana was not a state—it was first part of the Nebraska Territory and later, the Idaho Territory. Rather than ease the nation's problems regarding slavery, the Western Territories only increased the arguments. The Supreme Court's *Dred Scott v. Sanford* decision made slavery legal in all territories. This angered the abolitionists. These events and feelings eventually led to the Civil War.

In 1865, the 13th Amendment abolished slavery in the United States.

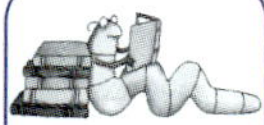

Word Definition

ABOLITIONIST: person who believed slavery was wrong and should be ended

Brother

The Civil War was fought between the American states. The argument was over states' rights to make their own decisions, including whether or not to own slaves. Some of the southern states began to secede (leave) the Union. They formed the Confederate States of America. Since Montana was not yet a state, it was not directly a part of the Civil War. In fact, Montana Territory was not established until 1864, one year before the end of the Civil War.

The Civil War

Word Definition

RECONSTRUCTION: the recovery and rebuilding period following the Civil War

vs. Brother

The Civil War was also called the War Between the States. Soldiers often found themselves fighting against former friends and neighbors, even brother against brother. Those who did survive often went home without an arm, leg, or both, since amputation was the "cure" for most battlefield wounds. More Americans were killed during the Civil War than during World Wars I and II together!

Get It In Writing!

1776
Declaration of Independence

1789
U.S. Constitution

1803
Louisiana Purchase incorporates eastern Montana into the U.S.

1889
Montanans ratify a state constitution; Congress gives its approval for statehood

1972
New state constitution is approved

WELCOME TO AMERICA!

People have come to Montana from other states and many other countries on almost every continent! As time goes by, Montana's population grows more diverse. This means that people of different races and from different cultures and ethnic backgrounds have moved to Montana.

In the past, many immigrants have come to Montana from midwestern and eastern U.S. states, Germany, Canada, Norway, Ireland, Wales, and England. More recently, people have migrated to Montana from Laos and Mexico. The mining town of Red Lodge has so many nationalities they host an annual Festival of Nations. However, compared to other states, Montana does not have a large number of immigrants.

Disasters & Catastrophes

1837

More than 10,000 Indians die from smallpox

1886–87

Severe blizzard kills tens of thousands of cattle

1917–20; 1929

Droughts and grasshoppers devastate Montana farms

1935

Helena is hit by earthquakes

1959

Earthquake creates Quake Lake on the Madison River

1988

Yellowstone National Park ravaged by wildfires

Legal Stuff

1870s

Miners' labor unions begin

1875

U.S. government orders Montana's Indians onto reservations

1910

Glacier National Park is created by the U.S. Congress

1924

Montana institutes a mining-license tax

1973

Montana passes the Strip Mine Reclamation Act and the Utility Siting Act

1863

Montana's first two schools are begun by Lucia Darling and Kate Dunlap

1916

Montana representative Jeannette Rankin becomes first woman elected to the U.S. Congress

1968

Jeannette Rankin leads 5,000 women on a war protest march in Washington, D.C.

Fight! Fight! Fight!

Wars that had an impact on Montana:

- **Revolutionary War**
- **War of 1812**
- **Civil War**
- **Indian Wars**
- **World War I**
- **World War II**
- **Korean War**
- **Vietnam War**
- **Persian Gulf War**

Custer's Last Stand

With many settlers coming to Montana, the Indians grew concerned. Some retreated to more remote areas, but others attacked settlers. U.S. Army troops were sent to Montana to protect the settlers and fight off the Indians. On June 25, 1876, a famous Indian battle occurred along the Little Bighorn River in Montana. U.S. Lieutenant Colonel George Armstrong Custer spotted a large encampment of thousands of Sioux, Cheyenne, and other Plains Indians. Custer, with less than 300 cavalrymen, marched to the Little Bighorn River to attack the Indians. He was hopelessly outnumbered and many question his motive for entering into a battle that his troops would most certainly lose. It took less than an hour for the thousands of Indian warriors to eliminate Custer's troops. One horse was the lone survivor of Custer's troops. The battle became known as Custer's Last Stand.

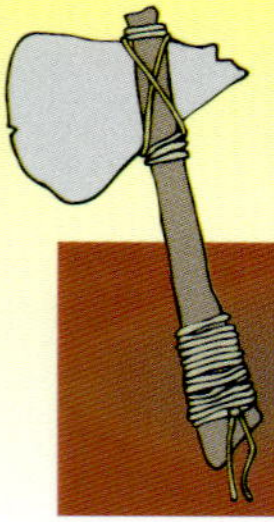

The Battle of Little Bighorn was led by great Indian leaders, Sitting Bull, Crazy Horse, and Gall.

Indian Tribes

Arapaho
Blackfeet
Crow
Cheyenne
Assiniboine

These tribes hunted bison to use for their meat, clothing, shelter, and tools. They made tepees from buffalo skins.

The Sioux came to Montana from the Dakotas to hunt.

Indian Tribes

Kootenai
Shoshone
Salish
Bannock

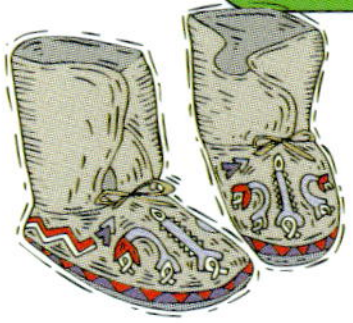

These tribes lived in Montana's Rockies. They hunted deer and bear. They also fished and gathered berries.

Here, There, Everywhere!

FRANÇOIS AND LOUIS DE LA VÉRENDRYE—French-Canadian brothers who were the first known non-Indians in Montana; hunted for new sources of furs

MERIWETHER LEWIS AND WILLIAM CLARK—sent by President Thomas Jefferson to explore lands in the West; assisted by Indian guide Sacagawea

MANUEL LISA—built Montana's first fur-trading post, named Fort Manuel

PIERRE JEAN DE SMET—Jesuit missionary who established St. Mary's Mission among the Salish; also worked with the Blackfeet

LIEUTENANT JOHN MULLAN—built a wagon road from the Columbia River to Fort Benton

JOHN BOZEMAN—trail blazer; cut trail from Wyoming to Virginia City, Montana, called the Bozeman Trail

DAVID THOMPSON—explorer, fur trader; explored and mapped western Canada and the American Northwest

Founding Fathers

MARCUS DALY—wealthy and powerful copper "king"; campaigned for his smelter town of Anaconda to be the capital; owned the *Anaconda Standard* newspaper

WILLIAM A. CLARK—wealthy and powerful copper "king"; pushed legislators to vote for Helena to be the capital; owned the *Butte Miner* newspaper; early state senator

SIDNEY EDGERTON—Montana's first territorial governor

JOSEPH K. TOOLE—Montana's first state governor

Founding Mothers

LUCIA DARLING—ran the school in Bannack, one of the first two schools in the state

KATE DUNLAP—ran the school in Nevada City, one of the first two schools in the state

MARY FIELDS—born a slave in Tennessee; moved to Montana in the 1880s and became a stagecoach driver; delivered mail for eight years in early Montana, becoming the second woman to deliver the U.S. mail

Famous American Indians

SITTING BULL—Sioux medicine man; took part in attack on U.S. troops at Battle of Little Bighorn

CRAZY HORSE—Sioux Indian chief; led successful attack on U.S. troops at Rosebud Creek and at Battle of Little Bighorn

CHIEF JOSEPH—Nez Percé Indian chief from Idaho; led march across Montana to escape relocation to a reservation; caught and forced to surrender only a short distance from safety of the Canadian border

PLENTY COUPS—Crow Indian leader; worked as scout for U.S. Army; represented American Indians at the dedication ceremony for the Tomb of the Unknown Soldier in Arlington, Virginia

SACAGAWEA—Shoshone Indian interpreter and guide who travelled with Meriwether Lewis and William Clark across the West with her infant son, Pompey, on her back

WHITE MAN RUNS HIM—Crow Indian who acted as a scout for George Armstrong Custer

BIG IGNACE—Canadian Iroquois who converted to Christianity; lived among Salish Indians in Montana

DID SOMEONE SAY BOO!?

BIGHORN BOOGEY MEN

At Little Bighorn Battlefield, site of Custer's Last Stand, there have been numerous sightings of dead soldiers, American Indian warriors, and even Custer himself.

SALOON SPOOK

At the Kelly Saloon in Garnet, there have been reports of ghostly piano music and sounds of people celebrating coming from the deserted building.

LADY IN WHITE

The Chico Hot Spring Lodge and Ranch in Pray is supposedly haunted by a Lady in White. She has been seen by both the staff and guests. In 1986, two security guards actually got a picture of her!

DO YOU BELIEVE IN GHOSTS?

Sports Stuff

ROBERT CRAIG KNIEVEL, otherwise known as "Evel Knievel," was born in Butte. He brought the circus spirit into the arena of sports with his daredevil motorcycle stunts. Jumping over things like buses and water fountains were his trademark. In 1974, he attempted to jump Idaho's Snake River Canyon but failed when his parachute opened early. He retired in 1981.

JERRY KRAMER, famous Green Bay Packer right guard, was born in Jordan. He was nominated for induction to the Pro Football Hall of Fame as a senior nominee in 1998, but was not accepted. He remains as one of the Packer's greatest right guards and most inspirational players.

JEAN FOSTER of Bozeman competed in the 2000 Olympics in Sydney in the area of shooting. She has won numerous shooting titles in the past, including the gold at Atlanta World Cup, silver at Milan World Cup, and the U.S. Championships.

Montanans enjoy an array of sports, from football to skiing, hockey to baseball, hunting to riding rodeo, fishing to snowmobiling—and the list goes on!

Entertainers

GARY COOPER—actor; famous for portraying strong, romantic heroes; won Academy Awards for performances in *Sergeant York* and *High Noon*

CHET HUNTLEY—TV news anchor; longtime news anchor for NBC

MYRNA LOY—actress; appeared in many films, including *The Thin Man* and *Cheaper by the Dozen*

THOMAS FRANCIS MCGUANE III—novelist and screenwriter; screenplays include *Two in the Shade* and *Missouri Breaks*

DANA CARVEY—comedian; star of *Saturday Night Live*; famous for his impression of President George Bush

MICHAEL SMUIN—choreographer

DIRK BENEDICT—actor

DAVID LYNCH—filmmaker

MARTHA RAYE—actress

GEORGE MONTGOMERY—actor

Authors

- A.B. GUTHRIE, JR.—novelist and playwright; famous for writing the script for *Shane*

- RICHARD BRAUTIGAN—novelist and essayist; first gained fame with his book *Trout Fishing in America*

- IVAN DOIG—journalist, novelist; his novel *This House of Sky* was nominated for a National Book Award in 1978

- DASHIELL HAMMETT—writer of detective novels including *Red Harvest* and *The Maltese Falcon*

- RICHARD HUGO—poet, essayist; works include the poetry collections *Lady Kicking Horse Reservoir* and *Making Certain It Goes On*

- DOROTHY JOHNSON—short-story writer, editor; her short story "The Man Who Shot Liberty Valance" was made into a movie

- WILLIAM KITTREDGE—novelist, short-story writer

- NORMAN FITZROY MACLEAN—writer, educator; famous for his novel *A River Runs Through It and Other Stories*

- WARREN EARLE STEGNER—novelist, short-story writer; received Pulitzer Prize in fiction for his novel *Angle of Repose*

- JAMES WELCH—novelist, poet

Artists

CHARLES M. RUSSELL—Montana's most popular painter and sculptor; created dramatic and sensitive portrayals of the history and culture of the West; famous for painting titled *Lewis and Clark Meeting Indians at Ross' Hole*, which hangs in the state capitol

EDGAR PAXSON—painter; created masterpiece known as *Custer's Last Stand*, which he worked on for 21 years

RALPH DECAMP—famous landscape painter; best-known work is titled *Gates of the Mountains*, which hangs in the state capitol

WILL JAMES—self-taught Western artist; wrote and illustrated books with action-packed drawings of cowboy life

EVELYN CAMERON—photographer; famous for photographs of Montana life in the late 1800s and early 1900s

HAROLD UREY—grew up in Montana; professor at many respected colleges throughout the country; discovered heavy water; helped develop the atomic bomb; studied the origins of planets; received Nobel Peace Prize in chemistry

MARTHA JANE "CALAMITY JANE" BURKE—frontierswoman, prospector; expert on shooting and riding; Army scout on Indian campaigns; later ran a restaurant in Castle

Very Important People

FOREST SERVICE SMOKEJUMPERS—brave men and women who risk their lives fighting forest fires across the country; based out of Missoula; parachute from planes with gear to fight hard-to-reach fires in the wilderness

MICHAEL MANSFIELD—served as U.S. representative, senator, Senate majority leader, and U.S. Ambassador to Japan; while in Congress, opposed the Vietnam War, fought to pass the Civil Rights Act of 1964, and to lower the voting age to 18

JEANNETTE RANKIN—social reformer; first woman U.S. representative; only member of Congress to vote against U.S. entry into both World Wars I and II; opposed American intervention in Vietnam

THOMAS JAMES WALSH—lawyer; U.S. senator who led the investigation of the Teapot Dome scandal; appointed U.S. attorney general by President Franklin D. Roosevelt, but died before taking office; first Montanan named to a cabinet post

BURTON KENDALL WHEELER—U.S. senator; ran for vice president on the Progressive Party ticket in 1924

BELLE FLIGELMAN—women's-rights activist; important in the campaign for women's right to vote in Montana; helped get Jeannette Rankin elected to Congress; supported national child labor laws and the right of women to serve on juries

Mountain Men

JIM BRIDGER worked as a fur trapper for the Rocky Mountain Fur Company. Bridger was a colorful Montana character—one story says that he was once wounded in the back by an arrowhead that stuck there for three years!

JOHN "LIVER-EATING" JOHNSON was a giant mountain man who enjoyed fur trapping. He married a Flathead Indian girl whose name meant "the swan." While away on a fur-trapping trip, Johnson's wife and unborn child were killed by Crow Indians. After that, he considered the Crow mortal enemies and vowed to kill any he came across. Johnson cut out their livers and rubbed the blood on his beard; that's how he got the nickname "Liver-Eating"!

JOHN COLTER was an explorer for the Lewis and Clark expedition. He later worked as a fur trapper. At one point, Colter was captured by the Blackfeet Indians. Instead of killing him outright, they stripped him of his clothes and allowed him a headstart to "run for his life." Amazingly, Colter outran the Indians and covered over 200 miles in a week, reaching Fort Manuel, barefoot, freezing, and starving!

The Plummer Gang

Henry Plummer and his bandit gang were driven out of Idaho into Montana. Here, Plummer posed as an intelligent, respectable citizen. He was elected sheriff of Bannack and then of neighboring Virginia City. Meanwhile, crime was running rampant in the two towns. Robberies and murders were increasing. No one knew their own sheriff was the mastermind behind these crimes!

A few of the citizens decided the sheriff was not helping to restore peace and order, so they formed a Vigilance Committee and decided to take the law into their own hands. Capturing one of the Plummer gang, they forced him to tell the names of the other members. Imagine their surprise when they learned that Henry Plummer, the sheriff, was the ringleader of the gang!

Plummer was asleep on the couch when the Vigilance Committee quietly caught him and walked him to the gallows. Henry Plummer and his numerous bandits were hanged for their crimes.

Keeping the Faith

St. Mary's Mission, Stevensville—descendant of first mission in the Northwest; established by Jesuit missionary Father de Smet for the Indians

St. Richard's Church, Columbia Falls—one of Montana's earliest Catholic churches

St. Ignatius Mission—dates back to 1864; organized by the Jesuit missionaries and Flathead Indians

St. Francis Xavier Church, Superior—dates back to 1892; contains beautiful stained-glass windows and elegant murals

St. Michael's Church, Missoula—built in 1863

B'Nai Israel Synagogue, Butte—oldest operating synagogue in the state

Cathedral of St. Helena, Helena—begun in 1907 and completed in 1924 ; has two large, red spires and Bavarian stained glass

SCHOOLS

University of Montana, Missoula
Montana State University, Bozeman
Eastern Montana College, Billings
Western Montana College, Dillon
Northern Montana College, Havre
College of Mineral Science and Technology, Butte
Carroll College, Helena
College of Great Falls, Great Falls
Rocky Mountain College, Billings

HISTORIC SITES

FORT UNION TRADING POST NATIONAL HISTORIC SITE, at North Dakota border near Sidney

GRANT-KOHRS RANCH NATIONAL HISTORIC SITE, near Deer Lodge

CHIEF PLENTY COUPS STATE HISTORIC PARK, Pryor—home and burial site of last chief of the Crow

PICTOGRAPH CAVE STATE HISTORIC SITE, southeast of Billings—preserves the remains of a prehistoric culture that existed in Montana 5,000 years ago

STATE PARKS

MISSOURI HEADWATERS STATE PARK, Three Forks—point where Lewis and Clark found that the Jefferson, Madison, and Gallatin rivers meet to form the Missouri River

MEDICINE ROCKS STATE PARK, Ekalaka—beautiful sandstone rocks; Indians considered it a holy place

Home, Sweet Home!

CONRAD MANSION, Kalispell—built in 1895; 3-story, shingle-style house

DALY MANSION, Hamilton—summer home of copper king, Marcus Daly; known as "Riverside" to the Daly family

COPPER KING MANSION, Butte—built in 1888 for William A. Clark

CASTLE, White Sulphur Springs—built in 1892 from stone quarried in the Castle Mountains

ORIGINAL MONTANA GOVERNOR'S MANSION, Helena—built in 1885 and home to nine Montana governors between 1913 and 1959

Home, Sweet Home!

MOSS MANSION, Billings—designed by architect of New York's famous Plaza Hotel

KLUGE HOUSE, Helena—unusual architecture of logs and half-timbering, with brick infil

BIELENBERG HOME, Deer Lodge—prairie-style house designed in 1910

GREENOUGH MANSION, Missoula—built in 1897 in the Queen-Anne style

Battles and Forts

A few of Montana's famous Battles

- **BIG HOLE NATIONAL BATTLEFIELD, Wisdom**—site of a major engagement of the Nez Percé War of 1877
- **ROSEBUD BATTLEFIELD, Decker**—site of the 1876 battle between the Sioux and General Crook's troops
- **CHIEF JOSEPH BATTLEFIELD, south of Chinook**—site where Chief Joseph of the Nez Percé surrendered after a six-day battle with U.S. Army troops in 1877

A few of Montana's famous Forts

- **FORT LOGAN, White Sulphur Springs**—post that defended the freight route to Helena, the mining operations at Confederate Gulch, and the cattle ranches in the river valleys
- **FORT KEOGH, southwest of Miles City**—at one time the largest cavalry post in Montana
- **OLD FORT BENTON, at Missouri riverfront in Fort Benton**—once a center of Missouri River commercial traffic
- **FORT MISSOULA**—built as protection from Flathead Indians
- **FORT PECK**—began as an Indian agency and trading post

Check out the following special Montana libraries! (Do you have a library card? Have you worn it out yet?!)

MONTANA STATE HISTORICAL SOCIETY LIBRARY, Helena—
special state research library

MONTANA STATE LAW LIBRARY, Helena

UNIVERSITY OF MONTANA LIBRARY, Missoula—
collections of Northwest history and law

MONTANA STATE UNIVERSITY, Bozeman—
collections of agriculture and science

BOZEMAN CARNEGIE LIBRARY—one of 2,800 free libraries funded by Andrew Carnegie

Rural libraries have grown in past years due to bookmobiles and interlibrary loans.

Attractions

GIANT SPRINGS, Great Falls—one of the largest freshwater springs in the world; noted by Lewis and Clark; nearby are Rainbow Falls and Great Falls, the largest waterfall on the Missouri River

VIRGINIA CITY—restored frontier mining town

BANNACK—ghost town whose mining-camp buildings still stand

FOSSIL BEDS, on Hell Creek north of Jordan—Site where paleontologists found an almost-complete skeleton of a *T. rex*

MONTANA TERRITORIAL PRISON, Deer Lodge—castlelike stone structure that served as the first territorial prison in the west

NATIONAL BISON RANGE, Moiese—grazing ground for one of the last bison herds in the U.S.

Museums

- C.M. RUSSELL MUSEUM COMPLEX, Great Falls
- MALMSTROM AIR FORCE MUSEUM AND AIR PARK, Great Falls
- MUSEUM OF THE PLAINS INDIANS, Shelby
- HERITAGE MUSEUM, Kalispell
- MIRACLE OF AMERICA STORY MUSEUM, Polson
- FLATHEAD INDIAN MUSEUM, St. Ignatius
- PIONEER MEMORIAL MUSEUM, Darby
- TOWE FORD MUSEUM, Deer Lodge
- NATIONAL GHOST TOWN HALL OF FAME MUSEUM, Anaconda
- MUSEUM OF THE ROCKIES, Bozeman
- HEADWATERS HERITAGE MUSEUM, Three Forks
- ALDER GULCH WORK TRAIN RAILROAD MUSEUM, Nevada City
- BEARTOOTH HISTORICAL MUSEUM, Columbus
- RANGE RIDER'S MUSEUM, Miles City
- PIONEER MUSEUM, Glasgow

Lest We Forget

CUSTER BATTLEFIELD NATIONAL MONUMENT, south of Hardin on the Crow Reservation— site of the Battle of Little Bighorn, also known as Custer's Last Stand

VIETNAM VETERANS' MEMORIAL, Butte— located in Stoddard Park

KOREAN VETERANS' MEMORIAL, Butte— located in Stoddard Park

LEWIS AND CLARK MEMORIAL, Fort Benton— bronze statue of the explorers and their Indian guide, Sacagawea

MISSOURI BREAKS NATIONAL MONUMENT, along the Missouri River—150-mile stretch along a free-flowing part of the Missouri River

The Arts

MARIAS MUSEUM OF HISTORY AND ART, Shelby

COPPER VILLAGE MUSEUM AND ARTS CENTER, Anaconda

GALLERY '85, Billings—features art of the pioneer West

C.M. RUSSELL GALLERY, Great Falls—exhibits the work of the Montana cowboy artist C.M. Russell

BILLINGS SYMPHONY ORCHESTRA

CASCADE QUARTET, Great Falls—classical and contemporary string quartet works

DILLON JUNIOR FIDDLERS—composed entirely of children who play violin

DAYSTAR, Great Falls—American Indian folklore dance-drama team

MONTANA REPERTORY THEATRE, Missoula

MONTANA BALLET COMPANY, Bozeman

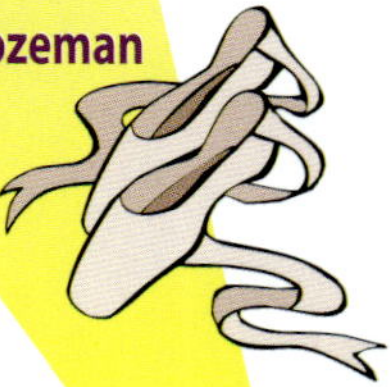

Montana is home to seven Indian reservations:

CROW INDIAN RESERVATION, Crow Agency—largest reservation in the state; home to most of the country's 8,500 Crow; host of the famous Crow Fair and Rodeo

BLACKFEET INDIAN RESERVATION, Browning—historically the largest and strongest Indian tribe in the state

ROCKY BOY INDIAN RESERVATION, Box Elder—home to the Chippewa and Cree Indians; features annual powwows

FORT BELKNAP INDIAN RESERVATION, Harlem—home to the Gros Ventre and Assiniboine tribes; annual events include Milk River Indian Days and Hays' Powwow

FORT PECK INDIAN RESERVATION, Poplar—home to around 6,000 Assiniboine and Sioux Indians; host the Wild Horse Stampede each July

FLATHEAD INDIAN RESERVATION, Pablo—home to the Salish and Kootenai tribes

NORTHERN CHEYENNE INDIAN RESERVATION, Lame Deer—includes historical sites such as graves of Indian chiefs and a bison jump; host Asland Powwow and the Lame Deer Northern Cheyenne Powwow

Roads,

Going-to-the-Sun Road, from St. Mary to Apgar through Glacier National Park

U.S. 89, from Yellowstone Park to Glacier National Park

Beartooth Highway, from Red Lodge to Yellowstone National Park on U.S. 212

and More,

Pompey's Pillar, east of Billings—massive sandstone pillar on which William Clark carved his name in 1806 while on his expedition with Meriwether Lewis; Clark named the pillar after Sacagawea's son, whom he had nicknamed "Pomp," meaning "little chief."

National Parks

Perhaps the most astounding and breathtaking parts of Montana are Yellowstone and Glacier National Parks. The magnificent scenery, incredible array of wildlife, and sheer size of the Rockies give these parks their grandeur.

Yellowstone National Park is located on the Wyoming border south of Livingston. Established in 1872, it is the oldest national park. Yellowstone boasts an area rich in gurgling mineral pools and erupting geysers. The park is reachable from Montana at three points.

Glacier National Park is located in northwestern Montana, near the Canadian border. It is a wonderland of glaciers, lakes, streams, waterfalls, forests, and wildlife. Visitors may cross the Continental Divide at Logan Pass on the Going-to-the-Sun Road that winds through Glacier.

Montana's Animals Include:

White-tailed Deer
Mule Deer
Elk
Black Bear
Grizzly Bear
Antelope
Bighorn Sheep
Mountain Goat
Moose
Caribou
Mountain Lion
Bison
Gray Wolf
Beaver
Lynx
Bobcat

Male bighorn sheep run into each other and ram heads to show which one is stronger.

Some endangered Montana animals are:

Whooping Crane

Bald Eagle

Black-footed Ferret

Grizzly Bear

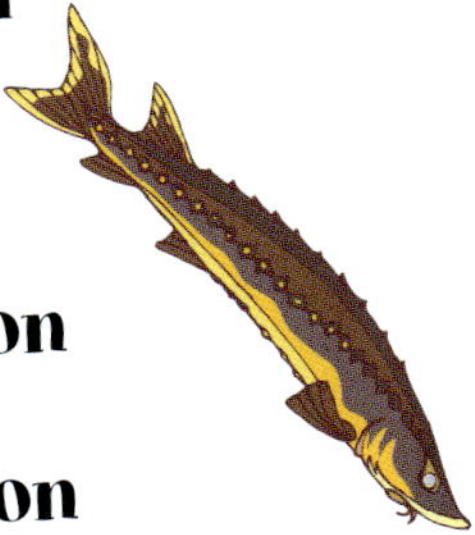

Gray Wolf

Pallid Sturgeon

White Sturgeon

There are less than 1,000 grizzlies in the lower 48 states. However, Alaska is home to around 31,000 grizzlies and brown bears!

Birds

You may spy these birds in Montana:

Bald Eagle
Peregrine Falcon
Kestrel
Hawk
Pheasant
Swan
Goose
Duck
Blackbird
Chickadee
Grouse
Meadowlark
Partridge
Magpie

An eagle's nest measuring 8 feet (2.4 meters) by 20 feet (6.1 meters) and weighing 4,000 pounds (1,814 kilograms) was once found in Glacier National Park!

Don't let these Montana bugs bug you!

Mayfly
Dragonfly
Grasshopper
Cricket
Water Bug
Whirligig Beetle
Ladybug
Tiger Swallowtail
Monarch Butterfly
Sphinx Moth
Mosquito
Honeybee
Bumblebee
Ant

Bumblebee

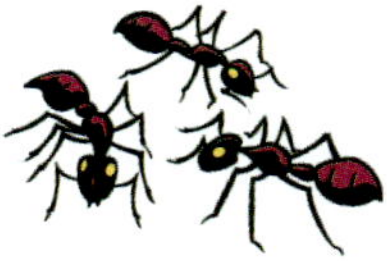
Ants

Monarch Butterfly

Dragonfly

Ladybug

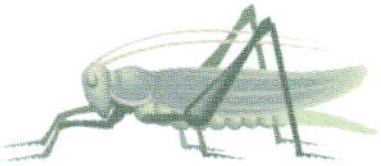
Grasshopper

Fish

Swimming in Montana's waters:

Walleye

Whitefish

Salmon

Yellow Perch

Grayling

Bass

Paddlefish

Sturgeon

Trout

Pond Critters

In Montana's ponds, you may find:

- Leech
- Crayfish
- Freshwater Mussel
- Fishing Spider
- Water Strider
- Diving Beetle
- Painted Turtle

Doctors once tried to cure patients by "bleeding" them with leeches!

Rocks and Minerals

Minerals are the building blocks of all rocks. Most minerals are tiny and you need a magnifying glass to see them clearly. Some minerals you may find in Montana include:

Tuff
Sandstone
Coal
Gneiss
Slate

Rocks are solid masses of minerals or rock fragments that occur in nature. Some rocks you may find in Montana include:

Iron Pyrite
Quartz
Calcite
Feldspar
Kaolinite
Mica

TREEMENDOUS!

THESE TREES TOWER OVER MONTANA:

ASPEN
ASH
BIRCH
COTTONWOOD
DOUGLAS FIR
SPRUCE
LODGEPOLE PINE
MOUNTAIN HEMLOCK
WESTERN RED CEDAR
WESTERN WHITE PINE
GRAND FIR
WESTERN TAMARACK
PONDEROSA PINE

Wildflowers

Glacier Lily
Aster
Shooting Star
Bear Grass
Bitterroot
Purple Coneflower
Wild Crocus
Buttercup
Balsamroot

Cream of the Crops

Agricultural products from Montana:

Beef Cattle

Feed Corn

Cherries

Wheat

Mustard

Apples

Barley

Sugar Beets

Dairy

Oats

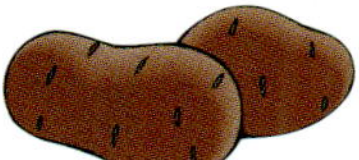
Potatoes

Hay

Beans

Sheep

Montana Potpourri

Montana has more than 100 **one-room schoolhouses**! Some have only four or five students!

World's greatest known **temperature change** in a 24-hour-period occurred in Browning, Montana. On January 23–24, 1916, the temperature dropped 100 degrees from 44°F (6.6°C) to -56°F (-49°C)!

Eureka calls itself the **Christmas Tree Capital of the World.**

The ***T. rex* skeleton** in New York City's American Museum of Natural History was found on a ranch in Montana.

Montana has several rodeos throughout the year. The **Montana Professional Rodeo Circuit Finals** are held at the state fair in Great Falls.

Butte, Montana, has been called the **Richest Hill on Earth** due to the large amounts of copper mined there.

The **largest snowflakes** ever recorded fell in Montana on January 28, 1887. They measured 15 inches (38 centimeters) across!

Celebrate!!!

CROW INDIAN FAIR, Crow Reservation—special time when the Crow recall their heritage; more than 1,000 tepees are raised for the week

WILD HORSE STAMPEDE, Fort Peck Indian Reservation—first stampede was held in 1901

LITTLE BIGHORN DAYS, Hardin—reenactment of Battle of Little Bighorn

BUCKING HORSE SALE, Miles City—events include a rodeo, dance, and livestock sale

FESTIVAL OF NATIONS, Red Lodge

MONTANA STATE FAIR, Great Falls

HELENA JAZZ FESTIVAL

BIG SKY MUSIC FESTIVAL, Missoula

NORTH AMERICAN INDIAN DAYS, Browning

Holidays

Calendar

Groundhog Day, *February 2*

Presidents' Day, *3rd Monday in February*

Memorial Day, *last Monday in May*

Battle of Little Bighorn Anniversary, *June 25*

Independence Day, *July 4*

Labor Day, *1st Monday in September*

Columbus Day, *2nd Monday in October*

Veterans Day, *November 11*

Thanksgiving, *4th Thursday in November*

During Montana's centennial celebration in 1989, an 1889 cattle drive was reenacted!

Montana is famous for...

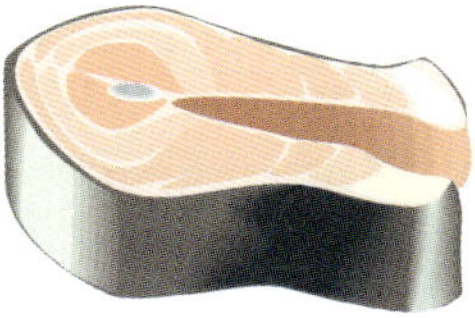

the following foods!

Broiled Walleye
Smoked Salmon
Buffalo Steak
Elk Steak
Lamb
Venison
Pheasant
Roast Duckling
Seared Mountain Trout
Jerk Steak Sandwich
Chuckwagon Beans
Home Fries

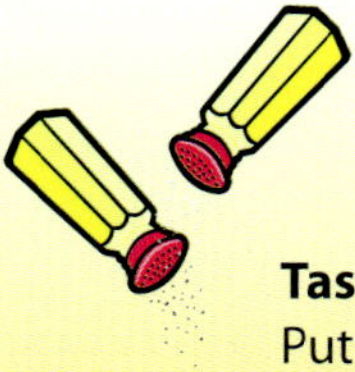

Tasty Trout
Put a trout filet on foil. Drizzle with lemon juice. Sprinkle with salt and pepper. Add shredded smoked ham and broil fish until done.

Montana Works!

Montana has a diverse economy that varies with each region. Southeastern Montana is a popular coal-mining area. This region also packs and ships many agricultural products, such as sugar beets, wheat, meat, and vegetables. Northeastern Montana has many wheat farms, ranches, and oil wells. It is one of the nation's top wheat-growing areas. Sheep and cattle are also raised in this region. Northwestern Montana is home to Malmstrom Air Force Base, which employs many people. Concrete and flour are made in this area also. Southwestern Montana is a big ranching area. It is also home to Helena, where food, bricks, and metals are made. Copper mining is still important to the Butte area.

Montana's tourism industry flourishes throughout the state but especially in the Rocky Mountain area of western Montana.

Books & Websites

My First Book About Montana by Carole Marsh
America the Beautiful: Montana by Ann Heinrichs
Kids Learn America by Patricia Gordon and Reed C. Snow
From Sea to Shining Sea: Montana by Judith and Dennis Fradin
Let's Discover the States: Montana by the Aylesworths
The Montana Experience Series by Carole Marsh

Montana Glossary

Glossary Words

atlatl: prehistoric tool used when throwing a spear

badlands: barren area in which rocks are eroded into awesome formations

bandit: a robber; member of a gang of outlaws

bison: a large plains mammal; also known as buffalo

bonanza: a source of great and sudden wealth

expedition: journey made for a specific purpose, as exploration

pishkun: high cliff

reservation: a tract of land set apart for American Indians

territory: a region of the U.S. not admitted as a state, but having its own legislature and an appointed governor

vigilante: any person who assumes the authority of the law, as to avenge a crime

Montana Spelling Bee

Here are some special Montana-related words to learn! To take the Spelling Bee, have someone call out the words and you spell them aloud or write them on a piece of paper.

Spelling Words

activist	**moccasin**
Bighorn	**mountain**
cavalry	**range**
continental	**reservation**
explore	**Sacagawea**
Gallatin	**sapphire**
glacier	**Sioux**
Helena	**trader**
heritage	**trapper**
Missoula	**Yellowstone**

ABOUT THE AUTHOR...

CAROLE MARSH has been writing about Montana for more than 20 years. She is the author of the popular *Montana State Stuff Series* for young readers and creator along with her son, Michael Marsh, of *Montana Facts and Factivities,* a CD-ROM widely used in Montana schools. The author of more than 100 Montana books and other supplementary educational materials on the state, Marsh is currently working on a new collection of Montana materials for young people. Marsh correlates her Montana materials to the Montana Standards for Social Studies. Many of her books and other materials have been inspired by or requested by Montana teachers and librarians.

EDITORIAL ASSISTANT:

Jill Sanders

GRAPHIC DESIGNERS:

Lisa Stanley Victoria DeJoy